AND MERELY TEACH

Irreverent Essays

on the Mythology of Education

Chaucer

And gladly wolde he lerne, and gladly teche.

THE PROLOGUE

Bliss Perry

Any teacher can study books, but books do not necessarily bring wisdom, nor that human insight essential to consummate teaching skill.

AND GLADLY TEACH: REMINISCENCES

John Dewey

We believe many things not because the things are so, but because we have become habituated through the weight of authority, by imitation, prestige, instruction, the unconscious effect of language, etc.

EXPERIENCE AND NATURE

Raymond P. Harris

A great deal of current writing on education contains generous amounts of an element I shall call the "folklore" of education. Such folklore . . . abounds in generalities, lacks reflection, is often without verifiable basis in fact, and makes no more useful contribution in education than it does in any other modern disciplines.

AMERICAN EDUCATION:
FACTS, FANCIES, AND FOLKLORE

AND MERELY TEACH

Irreverent Essays

on the Mythology of Education by

ARTHUR E. LEAN

Foreword by GEORGE S. COUNTS

Southern Illinois University Press
Carbondale and Edwardsville

Feffer & Simons, Inc.
London and Amsterdam

To George S. Counts

Mentor, colleague, friend

Why, man, he doth bestride this narrow world
Like a Colossus, and we petty men
Walk under his huge legs and peep about
To find ourselves dishonorable graves.

Foreword

By George S. Counts

> *He who can, does; he who cannot, teaches!*
> GEORGE BERNARD SHAW

> *He who can do, does; he who can think, teaches!*
> GEORGE BERNARD SHAW (*later*)

I AM VERY GLAD to write the foreword to this scholarly, brilliant, and challenging volume. As its pages demonstrate, Arthur Lean is a "maverick," that is, an unbranded person, a distinguished educator who is in bondage to no one.

This, of course, is what our country and world need in the present fateful age. The idea was brilliantly expressed a generation ago by Anne O'Hare MacCormick of *The New York Times*, one of our best informed and most perceptive commentators on the condition of man. In her column, following the signing of the Munich Pact in the early autumn of 1938, she stated that "all of those things are happening in the world that could not happen." These words constitute one of the most penetrating and challenging observations about the world in which we live. Perhaps it should be inscribed over the door of every school in the land. Mrs. MacCormick knew, of course, that things don't happen that can't happen. She was merely employing a literary figure to dramatize the obvious fact that so many things are happening that could not happen if our premises about the world were sound. In a word, we continue, in the agelong tradition of the human race, to think from premises derived from a world that has passed or is passing away. Or, to employ John Kenneth Galbraith's terms, we are being guided by the "conventional wisdom," that is, the wisdom of yesterday.

Dr. Lean is asking us to pass in critical review our current educational ideas and practices. Although we have made many gestures and shouted many slogans during the past decade, we have not actually come to grips with the great and inescapable task of rearing the young to live in the world of today and tomorrow. We should never forget the observation made some years ago by Henry Steele Commager in his *The American Mind:* "The decade of the nineties is the watershed of American history"—a watershed between an "America predominantly agricultural" and an "America predominantly urban and industrial." We should also turn our minds to the warning of another of our distinguished historians, Carl Bridenbaugh, president of the American Historical Association in 1963. In his inaugural address he declared without qualification: "It is my conviction that the greatest turning point in all human history, of which we have any record,

Foreword

has occurred within the twentieth century." And
then he added, "It now appears probable that mid-
nineteenth century America or Western Europe had
more in common with fifth century Greece . . .
than with their own projections into the middle of
the twentieth century." Indeed, as Norman Cousins
observed when we entered the atomic age, "Modern
man is obsolete."

Let us hope that this volume will be widely read
and that it will stimulate creative thinking, not only
by members of the profession, but also by lay citizens who are concerned about the prospects of our
American democracy—including members of school
boards. Let us proceed, therefore, to rear a generation of mavericks, a generation capable of grappling
boldly, intelligently, and creatively with our swiftly
changing world. Let us study the history of education in cultural perspective for the purpose of find-
ing out, not only what we should do, but also what
we should not do.

Preface

A teacher affects eternity; he can never tell where his influence stops.

HENRY BROOKS ADAMS

[Teaching] seems to me beyond doubt the greatest of the professions.

THEODORE BRAMELD

THIS LITTLE BOOK represents my attempt to express the distillation of many ideas about education—ideas developed during most of a lifetime spent in and about schools. This is a highly personal document, much of it controversial and iconoclastic; some readers will feel reinforced, while others will be irritated, perhaps even infuriated—just as many of us tend to be upset when our pet prejudices and "sacred cows" are exposed and challenged. But let there be no doubt about my sincerity of purpose: I believe that education is of supreme importance to the welfare and prosperity of our country and of the world, and I believe that at present education is not nearly as good as it should be and must be, and that a "great reappraisal" is needed.

Those Pollyannas who feel that ours is the best of all possible educational worlds will doubtless remonstrate that I am too "negative," too critical, that the situation couldn't possibly be that bad. To them I can only reply that it is probably considerably worse, that we are indeed facing a crisis whose scope and intensity we have not yet begun to appreciate.

Why should "the noblest of all professions" suffer from an increasing shortage of qualified personnel? Why do we read more and more about "teacher dropouts"? The many attractions and rewards of teaching are too numerous and well known to need repetition here, but unless the American people proceed with vigor and dispatch to improve working conditions and raise salaries for teachers at all levels, the crisis will continue to grow and to assume the proportions of a national catastrophe.

I believe, with Horace Mann, that the "common" (i.e., *public*) school is the greatest discovery ever made by man. I believe in public education, provided in public schools for all the children of all the people. I believe, with Lawrence A. Cremin, that "If . . . growing numbers of citizens can be convinced of the need to approach 'the great reappraisal' with a deepening sense of the crucial relationship between public education and the future of America, the gains may be truly significant."

It would be impossible for me to name all those to whom I am indebted for counsel and suggestions in the preparation of this volume. I would certainly be

Preface

remiss, however, if I did not express my appreciation to those teachers, colleagues and friends who have so strongly influenced my thoughts and attitudes, and with whom I share whatever credit might accrue from the effect of this book: George S. Counts, George E. Axtelle, Claude A. Eggertsen, Leonard V. Koos, Harold R. W. Benjamin, John E. Grinnell, and the late W. C. Bagley. Especial thanks go to my old friend Charles Follo, who has steadfastly encouraged me to write this book, and to John L. Childs, B. J. Kelley, and John E. Warriner, who read most of the manuscript and made many valuable suggestions. I am grateful also to Elmer J. Clark, Dean of the College of Education of Southern Illinois University, for continued cooperation and assistance.

Two of these essays, "Professor vs. Student" and "The Eradication of Misinformation," originally appeared in *School and Society* and are reprinted here with permission.

Southern Illinois University
February 9, 1968   *Arthur E. Lean*

Contents

AND MERELY TEACH

Irreverent Essays

on the Mythology of Education

PUBLISHED
WORKS

Education as Commodity

The tragic thing about American education is that by avoiding ultimate questions and concentrating on how to get loaves and fishes, the schools and colleges make out of our youngsters precisely what their parents wish them to become.

BERNARD IDDINGS BELL:
Foreword to And Madly Teach *by* MORTIMER SMITH

The school failures I found [on an extensive visitation trip] were monotonously not the failures of our professional educators. They were the deeper failures of our total society pressing in upon the classrooms.

ROBERT LEWIS SHAYON

EDUCATION TODAY IS BIG NEWS. More than ever before in the history of our country, it is a matter of national concern. It pervades our newspapers, magazines, television and radio programs. It is the subject of much legislation, of massive federal grants to support such projects as "Head Start," "Upward Bound," "Higher Horizons," international education, encouragement of research, use of automation, and so on. For the first time in the history of the United States, both our President and Vice-President are former teachers, and emphasis on education is an outstanding aspect of their administration.

A large amount of publicity about education appears in the mass media, but unfortunately most of it comes from the wrong people—from journalists, commentators, the military, "ax-grinders." Too often these publicists understand only superficially the scope and complexity of the great public enterprise of education; nor do they understand its inevitable expression of the underlying culture. But, even more unfortunately, among the supposed specialists— those people professionally engaged in education— far too many are distressingly naïve and inclined to oversimplify the character of the very enterprise in which they are engaged.

Much of this confusion and ambivalence arises from our tendency to regard education as a commodity. When we want a loaf of bread or a carton of milk, we go to the grocery store for it. When we

4

Education as Commodity

want "education," we go to school for it. Just as the grocery store purveys food, we think the school purveys education. When the father asks his son, "What did you learn in school today?" he expects a definite, substantive answer. If the son replies, "I learned that 2 plus 2 equals 4," the father is satisfied.

This concept of education as a packaged and wrapped commodity long ago became a stereotyped attitude in our society; indeed, it began to develop soon after institutions called "schools" were established to provide for the formal instruction of the young and to induct them into the culture. As a result, over the years we have indoctrinated ourselves with the notion that *education is what goes on in schools*. "Finish your education before you get married," parents tell their children. "To get a good job, get a good education," we hear repeatedly on our television receivers.

We really know better, of course. In our more reflective moments we readily admit that many of our most vivid and effective learning experiences are not part of a deliberately organized instructional program, and that many of them take place far from "school." Furthermore, we know that the infant begins to learn soon after birth and continues to learn, for better or worse, for several years before he begins to attend school.* We also realize that

* "Schooling is a part of the work of education, but education in its full meaning includes all the influences that go to form the attitudes and dispositions (of desire as well as of belief), which constitute dominant habits of mind and character." JOHN DEWEY

these early learnings are some of the most important in life.

College undergraduates, to be sure, have for many years spoken sophisticatedly about not letting their courses and textbooks "interfere" with their college education. When a Columbia University professor stated recently that "the dominant influences on most American college students are not their courses, nor their books and lectures—but their fellow students," he was only emphasizing what is generally known, but largely ignored, by professors and administrators, as well as by the general public.

In like manner, we read in our newspapers that a proposed state system of commuter junior colleges will make college available to more people at lower rates by saving room and board costs—the major expense of college education—and that college education will thus be made cheaper for the taxpayer because the state will not have to provide the "dormitories and other non-educational facilities" needed on campuses where students live. Most people would read such a statement without blinking an eye, but the Columbia professor quoted above would contend—and I am sure that all of us who have ever lived in a dormitory would have to agree—that the experience of dormitory living is one of the most effective educational experiences we have ever had, and that what we learned there far outlives most courses and classroom memories.

It is not only our concept of education which is superficial and imprecise, to be sure. Many other terms in common, everyday use—terms such as "democracy," "communism," "religion," "progressive education"—are used in the same uncritical way. The United States Supreme Court has had, and still has, extreme difficulty in attempting to develop a clear, unambiguous definition of "obscenity." People characteristically go through life complacently employing vague, indefinite catchwords and phrases as substitutes for logical thinking.

But the fundamental mistake we make which is responsible, more than anything else, for our confused thought about education is our failure to recognize the inescapable way in which it is connected with the culture which creates it and which it serves. In our naïve association of education only with schools we ignore its complex, protean character, its ubiquitous pervasiveness. We persist in efforts to isolate and quantify it, to "scientize" it, and all these efforts are doomed to failure.

In fine, our thought about education will continue to be confused as long as we think of it as a commodity strongly identified with the development of "marketable skills." Education is not exclusively a school undertaking, and the school, moreover, does not have a life of its own, independent of the culture. Small wonder, then, that the impression created by so much of the publicity about education today is that of the blind leading the blind, of confusion thrice confounded. It is to recognize the existence of this confusion, to bring it to light, to analyze its elements and, hopefully, to suggest some remedies, that I have written this book.

DO!
THINK!

2

Education as Cognition

Greeting his pupils, the master asked:
    What would you learn of me?
And the reply came:
    How shall we care for our bodies?
    How shall we rear our children?
    How shall we work together?
    How shall we live with our fellowmen?
    How shall we play?
    For what ends shall we live?
And the teacher pondered these words, and sorrow
was in his heart, for his own learning touched not
these things.

CHAPMAN AND COUNTS

. . . we simply fall from one formalism into an-
other, from one dung-hill of inert ideas into another.

ALFRED NORTH WHITEHEAD

FOR MANY YEARS NOW, self-styled "scholars" in higher education have been critical of teachers in the lower schools for not "knowing their stuff" well enough, for being deficient in mastery of their teaching fields. Clearly, such criticism is open to question, for have not these elementary and high school teachers learned their "subjects" from the very professors who are doing the complaining?

Certainly there are unfortunate cases of misassignment, such as the classic one of the young man who, on reporting for his first teaching post in a small high school, was assigned to teach a class in Latin. When he protested to the principal that he had never studied Latin, the administrator answered, "I know it, but you're the only one available. Here's a copy of the textbook; you have this weekend to get ready." When the class met for the first time the following Monday, the young man asked how many of the pupils already had any knowledge of Latin. Receiving no response, he held up the book and said, "Well, neither have I, but I'm on page 10. Catch me if you can."

Obviously, teachers need to be well-grounded in their teaching fields; to argue otherwise would be asinine. But the problem is bigger than that. Over the years it has been pointed out by school administrators, placement directors, board members, and others that when elementary and secondary school teachers (especially the latter) have job trouble, become disgruntled and drop out of the profession as failures, their problems in the great majority of cases arise not because they don't "know their stuff" but rather out of their inability to handle the classroom situation. Problems of "discipline," control, maintenance of a proper atmosphere in the classroom, personality adjustment—these are the predominant causes of teacher drop-outs.

This is perhaps the main reason why the typical professor in the typical college or university can contribute very little except a "horrible example" to those of his students who are preparing to teach. For the usual college class is a lecture, a "one-way street," with the professor on the dispensing end and the students—often largely somnolescent * —on the receiving end. (How often students have remarked, "This professor seems to know his stuff, but he certainly *doesn't* know how to put it across"!) But the problem of communication is seldom recognized; there is little provision for the great values of discussion, of dialectic, of helping students to learn from each other. The erudite professor, of course, would *never* admit that even he might learn from his students if he ever gave them a chance to express their ideas, ask questions, interpret to each other and to him, and so on—to do anything, in short, but answer his questions at quiz time.

No; the college student becomes more and more inured to the stereotype of education as material set out to be "covered"—that is, memorized, recalled and regurgitated on demand. In college there are no "discipline problems" to speak of; uninterested, un-

* Students' definition of a professor: One who talks in other people's sleep.

motivated but long-suffering students simply go to sleep—mentally, at least—or "cut" the class as often as possible.

The recently appointed liberal arts dean, formerly a science professor, at a large university was quoted as declaring: "The ultimate object of a college education should be the acquisition of knowledge, and this must have priority." Lest I be misunderstood, let me repeat most earnestly that I should not be misinterpreted by my readers as advocating that substantive knowledge is not important. It *is* important, of course, but it is only one aspect of the total educative experience and should not be emphasized to the exclusion of the myriad of ideas, attitudes, appreciations which are ignored under the conventional system of lecture, read, and test recall.

Education, to be effective, requires that some *change* take place in the educand; he must be different, in some way, as a result of the learning experience. "Knowing more" is one kind of change, to be sure, but mere information is quickly forgotten unless continuously used; and the complex realm of personality development—attitudes, appreciations, moral and esthetic sensibilities, and so on—is far more important than ability to recite a multiplication table without an error.

Hence, our almost exclusive preoccupation with the cognitive aspects of education in our schools, and our corresponding neglect of other and often far more important affective and conative aspects, result in the sterility and meaninglessness so commonly found in our many educational "disaster areas."

12

3

The "Mere Task of Teaching"

*Many of our "teachers" are not really teachers.
They are mathematicians, physicists, historians,
linguists, etc.,—not teachers. Many of them are men
(and women) of great stature; major contributors
to science, technology, and the arts; but they are
not teachers. On some scales of worth to humanity
they outweigh the teachers; but they are not
teachers. They might even be indispensable to
institutions of higher learning; but they are not
teachers. To them, students are means; to teachers,
students are the end products,—all else is a means.
Hence there is but one interpretation of high
standards in teaching: standards are highest where
the maximum number of students—slow learners
and fast learners alike—develop to their maximal
capacity.*

JOSEPH SEIDLIN

*Another reason for substandard teaching simply is
that college professors don't know how to teach.
Aside from a microscopic number who have had
some experience in grade or high schools (where
formal teacher training is required), nobody on
the typical campus has ever had a lesson in learning
theory, lecturing techniques, or organization of
material for classroom presentation.*

JOHN FISCHER

AN ADVERTISING PAMPHLET recently received from a prominent publisher of books in professional education depicts on its front page a young lady, obviously a teacher, sitting head in hands at her desk and gazing thoughtfully down at the papers spread out before her. The caption under the picture reads: ". . . prepares the beginning teacher for a variety of responsibilities *beyond the mere task of teaching itself. . . .*" (italics added)

Now, any time we conceive of teaching as a "mere task," we are in deep trouble, for good teaching is certainly one of the finest of fine arts, as well as one of the most difficult. Complex, many-sided, elusive, it is all too rarely found in our schools, especially at the level which we pompously misname "higher education." In many years as student, teacher, administrator, and classroom observer, I have seen much fine teaching in elementary schools, considerably less in secondary schools; and as for the undergraduate college level, a good deal of what passes for "teaching" there is little short of a national disgrace.

Our fuzziness and confusion about the nature of teaching is demonstrated in many ways. There is a long-standing stereotype in higher education setting the "scholar" apart from the "teacher," as if the two functions were mutually exclusive. The scholar-stereotype emphasizes research and publication; thus, recently a well-known university was crit-

The "Mere Task of Teaching"

icized in the press for "paying too much attention to scholarly work and not enough to teaching." *Ergo*, teaching is not scholarly work! And not long ago at another university a young professor's appointment was terminated because, as the president explained, he had performed adequately in the classroom but had not made sufficient scholarly contribution. *Ergo*, adequate classroom performance does not constitute scholarly contribution!

As long as we thus exclude teaching from our interpretation of the nature of scholarly work, we shall necessarily perpetuate the caricature which now passes for teaching in so many of our classrooms. What we desperately need in education at all levels today is that combination which William C. Bagley many years ago called the "scholar-teacher," but such a union is *rara avis* indeed.

Likewise, a few years ago another university sought a federal grant to expand its in-service work program so that university students might get jobs in nearby public schools doing "such non-instructional work as grading papers, supervising playgrounds and assisting the regular teacher in preparation of class work." Now, if these listed activities constitute "non-instructional work," I will cheerfully eat my mortarboard.

"Good teaching is not only a relatively private performance, but it resists measurement," says a recent report of the Carnegie Foundation for the Advancement of Teaching. And although administrators commonly make pious speeches about "rewarding good teaching" by their faculty members, academic promotions and prestige—as well as salary increments—actually depend primarily upon books and articles published, papers read at scholarly conferences, and research grants. What matter if the publications are ineffably trivial in their significance, if the speeches are so specialized and dull that they put even their sophisticated audiences to sleep, if the research grants predictably produce nothing of consequence? That's the way the academic ball bounces!

When administrators in higher institutions recruit new faculty members, they almost never betray the slightest interest in the teaching ability of the prospect, but they pay great attention to his list of publications.

Relief from teaching has become a status symbol in our universities; appointments carrying light teaching loads—or no teaching at all—are much sought after and flaunted with great pride. This "flight from teaching" is due also, although almost nobody admits it, to the professor's sublimated guilt-complex about his incompetence as a teacher. Very few people can remain indefinitely comfortable and complacent while daily demonstrating their utter inadequacy in the job for which they are being paid, and monthly drawing their salaries under false pretenses. As a matter of fact, many young Ph.D.'s nowadays take lucrative jobs with industry, government, and research institutes, while the rest head for the institutions whose light teaching loads allow them maximum time for the research and writing upon which their future advancement depends.

The "Mere Task of Teaching"

One of the most commonly heard assumptions about university teaching goes like this: Undergraduate students suffer from being taught in large lecture sections or discussion groups by graduate assistants instead of regular professors. These graduate assistants (so the argument goes) are usually young, inexperienced and much more interested in their own doctoral studies than in the low-prestige activity of teaching undergraduates, so the quality of their teaching is much lower than that of the professors. In mouthing this generalization we overlook something very important: in their "teaching," these young graduate assistants conform to the dominant pattern; they teach as they have been taught by their professors, and if those same professors neither know nor care about good teaching, what can be expected from the teaching done by graduate assistants but more of the same miserable performance?

Actually, some departments attempt to schedule discussion sections in order to get away from the deadly monotony of constant lecturing, but here again (so say the students) the result is usually failure. The students are so accustomed to being "talked at" that they find it difficult to speak up when given an opportunity. Rarely is the instructor skilled in stimulating discussion; on the contrary, he often delights in greeting with elaborate sarcasm any comment or question advanced by a curious or highly motivated student (especially if the instructor doesn't know the answer and of course doesn't want to admit it) and often the brash student wishes he'd never opened his mouth. An atmosphere of frustration settles over the class, and the instructor in desperation starts to lecture or dismisses the group after reprimanding them for being so "apathetic" and "uninterested in learning"!

Fortunately, the quality of teaching tends to be considerably higher in the so-called "lower schools," especially in the much-maligned elementary grades which are the most important of the child's life. A good start in those early years is of incalculable benefit for future progress. Elementary-school teaching is a relatively low-prestige activity because of the traditional mistaken notion that "anybody can teach the three R's to little children." If you think that's so, just try it sometime!

Professor vs. Student

*The general attitude in higher education today is
one of student* vs. *faculty, rather than student* with
faculty.

ANONYMOUS STUDENT

*We could get something done around here if it
weren't for these blankety-blank students!*

ANONYMOUS PROFESSOR

THIS PITIFUL PROFESSORIAL PLAINT, oft quoted in academic circles, points up a curious anomaly which has impressed more than one observer of the American educational scene. Although it seems fairly obvious to most educators that the teacher's role should be, above all else, a *helping* one, many good teachers are traumatized repeatedly by displays of pedagogical disdain and superciliousness on the part of their colleagues toward those very individuals who are, after all, the *raison d'être* of the entire educational enterprise.

This lamentable state of affairs may be found most commonly (though by no means exclusively) at the college and university undergraduate level. Here the range of professorial attitudes toward the objects of their endeavors runs the gamut from outright contempt and derision through amused tolerance to genuine respect. But there is sufficient faculty representation at the former end of the scale to furnish a disquieting spectacle.

Such ignoble feelings are, to some extent, a reaction to the modern trend toward excessive sentimentality which—in the opinion of many, at any rate— has accompanied an overemphasis upon "child-centeredness" in education. One of the more reactionary exponents of this group was the late (and possibly unlamented) Latin professor who regarded with a jaundiced eye the current tendency to emphasize the importance of knowing the "whole student," including his personality traits, family background,

Professor *vs.* Student

extracurricular interests, and so on. This particular professor each semester would fix incoming classes with a baleful glare and sternly admonish them: "I don't know who you are, and I don't want to know. I'm not in the least interested in your private lives or your doings outside of this classroom. Just be here at the appointed time, recite when you're called upon, and you'll get your 'C' at the end of the course." Could it be that this misanthropic attitude on the part of a genuine scholar has had something to do with the steady decline in the study of classical languages?

The "sink or swim" treatment is not at all uncommon in universities. Some professors make it a point to maintain a forbidding reserve toward students. Speculating upon the motives behind this practice, one might identify a basic feeling of inadequacy beneath an overtly expressed disinclination to be bothered by silly questions and apple-polishing.

Availability of professors for conferences with students is often limited to one or two hours a week, and even these schedules are sometimes disregarded in the most cavalier fashion by faculty members.

In certain institutions, amazingly enough, there is a well-recognized and publicly expressed "weed 'em out" policy which manifests itself in a deliberate attempt to banish large numbers of students after they have been admitted. This practice probably occurs most often in state universities required by law to admit all graduates of accredited high schools in the state. It also is found in certain types of specialized and professional programs. The military ruthlessness and callous indifference of such policies

contrast strangely with the current national emphasis upon the conservation and best utilization of
human resources.

Although this "kick the students around" attitude is certainly not confined to institutions of
higher education, it is probably much less common
in the lower schools. One highschool teacher, after
visiting university freshman classes being attended
by some of his former students, was visibly shaken
by the experience and later commented to a professor friend, "If we taught them in high school as you
do here, we'd lose our jobs in a hurry—and right-
fully so."

This entire generalized attitude of teacher vis-á-
vis student is easily rationalized by equating it with
maintenance of academic standards. College professors and administrators are typically almost patho-
logically sensitive about academic respectability.
And here we are presented with a situation which
reminds us of the smear techniques of recently notorious politicians. Whenever a new educational proposal is made, be it in curriculum, evaluation, ad-
missions policies, or any other area, opponents often
can effectively quash it by claiming that its adoption
would "lower standards." Usually no real proof is
required; the charge alone suffices; the proposal becomes a "dead duck."

There is much loose talk about standards, and
often the most voluble users of the term would be
hard pressed to define it save in terms of superimposed requirements and of relatively meaningless
phrases, such as "solid, substantial work." Now, no

educator in his right mind would deny the value and importance of achievement. At the same time, however, much has been accomplished in the study of the learning process and the optimum conditions under which learning takes place. Unfortunately, some of our most learned teachers either are ignorant of all this or they deliberately disregard or violate it.

Many a toiler in the educational vineyard has remarked upon the spectacle of professors who seem to assume that the institution which they serve exists primarily for them and their convenience, and only incidentally for the students, who are treated as "the lowest form of college life." But, obviously, the faculty members are at once the employees and, in a sense, the *servants* of those students. There is no room in the teaching profession at any level for practitioners who believe that students are a necessary evil and a backward, inferior lot; that respect and concern for students is somehow a sign of weakness; that pomposity and superciliousness toward students is, after all, no more than they deserve. Unfortunately, there are more than a few teachers who seem convinced that anything more than a mere mechanical, routine effort on their part is "soft pedagogy"; that deliberate obscurantism, trickery, cheating, and all sorts of unethical practices by the teacher are actually laudable and perfectly legitimate aspects of the educative process; and that the best way to maintain academic respectability and high scholastic standards is to make it as difficult as possible for students to learn anything.

TEST TEST TEST
A
C
B
A
F

5

The Farce Called "Grading"

A sustained effort should be made to throw out false inducements to learning. In one way or another most of these refer to our obsession with grades. A few colleges that have ended the grading system, like those truly brave ones that have thrown out faculty ranks, have shown what can be done. It is possible to interest students in intrinsic learning, once we rid ourselves of the ancient hobby of making book on each performance. Grades may be useful for checking the memory of items of fact or the solving of pat mathematical problems. As a system for evaluating attainment of broad educational aims, it remains a failure. Few teachers have any systematic idea of how to grade fairly. Grading is also the chief villain behind the scandal of college cheating.

LOUIS T. BENEZET

I have long ago reached the conclusion that the marking system itself is damaging in its impact on the education of our children and youth, and that it should go the way of the hickory stick and dunce caps. It should be abandoned at all levels of education.

ERNEST O. MELBY

OF ALL THE COMMON PRACTICES in our schools, doubtless the most tyrannical and indefensible is our insistence on attempting to evaluate students' performance through a system of grades or "marks." The harm done by this practice is incalculable, but we persistently cling to it in spite of its obvious unworkability. Every person who has ever gone to school can cite numerous instances of unfairness and injustice caused by grading systems and practices, but for some strange reason we seem to assume it to be necessary and intrinsic to the process of formal education.

Some years ago, when numerical grading on a percentage basis was more common than today, several experiments were conducted in an attempt to determine how precisely teachers could evaluate students' written work. In one well-known study, in order to "prejudice the garden to roses," an *exact* subject was chosen—mathematics, of course, because in that field, as everybody knows, things are either right or wrong—and a panel of experienced mathematics teachers, recognized by their peers for their competence, was assembled to do the evaluating. Student papers in plane geometry were graded by these expert teachers, each using an identical copy so as to eliminate any persuasive effect of extraneous factors such as neatness. The result was, of course, that the grades assigned to exactly the same paper ranged all the way from the 90's down to the

The Farce Called "Grading"

40's and 50's. And this in an *exact* subject where answers are "either right or wrong"! Similar results were obtained in other comparable studies.

The shift to letter-grading with fewer distinctions (the familiar A, B, C, D, with either E or F to designate failure) has not really solved the problem; it has merely reduced the number of categories (whereupon, of course, we promptly proceed recidivistically to attach plus and minus signs—multiple ones if single ones will not suffice). And of course we *must* have an equivalency table to indicate that "A" includes the range 93–100 or 90–100, "B" 85–92 or 80–89, and so on down, refusing in our obstinacy to recognize the fatal inconsistency involved: is "A" 93 or 100 or something in between? How about 95? 98? 96.123456789?

During the hectic post-World War II days I was pressed into service to teach Freshman Composition (Expository Writing) at a large university. There were more than a hundred sections of this course, each with a maximum of twenty-five students. We used a book of readings as a basis for class discussion and weekly themes. In addition to class sessions, each student had a short fortnightly conference with his instructor to go over his work and discuss ways of improving his written expression.

One of the "full" professors in the English department was in charge of all the teaching in this course, and he regularly convened the instructors—some seventy or eighty of them—for purposes of coordination and standardization of instruction. Usually at these sessions we were given identical copies of an actual student theme which had been selected at random and duplicated exactly as originally submitted. We took thirty to forty minutes to read and evaluate this short theme, whereupon we wrote on it a grade and an evaluative comment. Having listed our names alphabetically on the blackboard, the professor in charge then called them one by one, and each instructor responded to his name by stating the grade he had assigned to that theme. This grade was inscribed after his name on the blackboard.

Invariably the assigned grades on the same theme ranged all the way from "A" (excellent) to "E" (failure). Those instructors who judged that theme to be in either of those extreme categories were then called upon to stand up and justify their grades. This they usually did with great earnestness and sincerity, albeit with increasing reluctance, for in the process their own personal biases, prejudices, and confusions were soon revealed for all to see. (It quickly became obvious to many neophyte instructors that "C-minus" was an inconspicuous, colorless grade which would not require them to expose themselves to the public justification-humiliation process.) Most of the assigned grades tended, of course, to cluster in the middle of the scale, but there were almost always some on the extremes. But not once did we stop to consider the *student* who must maintain a certain minimum grade-average to stay in school, and whose mark on that theme might be "A" or "E" depending on which instructor he has!

All of us are familiar with the classic examples of

The Farce Called "Grading"

students' submitting the same paper to different instructors (or even to the same instructor at different times!) and getting widely varying grades, of handing in obscure works of famous authors and getting them back marked "failure," and so on.

Grading tends to stigmatize and punish the less able student, who may be trying very hard but, through no fault of his own, simply did not inherit much in the way of native intelligence.

In spite of the staggering amount of incontrovertible evidence that grading not only does not accomplish its purpose but in reality inhibits and injures the educative process, we obstinately continue with this perverted practice.

After all, what is a "grade" supposed to be and do? Perhaps we could get general agreement on the statement that it is a symbol purporting to express a measurement of academic achievement—an evaluation of the quality and quantity of learning. Now, in order to measure anything, we need a standard such as a ruler or tapeline for linear measurement, a scale for measuring weight, and so on. By using such standards I can determine that the desk at which I sit is 30 inches high, and that its surface measures 28 inches by 20 inches. I put my portable typewriter on a scale and determine its weight to be nine pounds. I look at the thermometer on the wall and discover that room temperature is 70 degrees Fahrenheit. Other people using the same standards would arrive at the same results; any variations would be infinitesimal and certainly negligible for practical purposes.

If all this be so, then what sense does it make for us to speak of "giving" a grade to a student, or of his "earning" or "deserving" it? Do I "give" my desk a height of 30 inches? Does my typewriter "earn" a weight of nine pounds? Does this room "deserve" a temperature of 70 degrees? Arrant nonsense, of course, but this ridiculous absurdity is exactly what we constantly do with our grading systems.

Compounding our criminal practices, we use grades for reward and punishment. Recently a coed sued her university because she claimed that her failing grade in one course was "unfair" and resulted from an attempt "to discipline and punish her" for alleged wrongful conduct. She asserted that she had been found innocent by the university's disciplinary committee, but that the instructor and administrative superiors to whom she had appealed had refused to "raise the grade" to the "B" which she said she had "merited." And this occurred in an institution of what we fancifully call "higher learning"!

When students disobey instructions or otherwise transgress (often unintentionally) we say to them, "Because of this, I am lowering your grade five points (or one letter)." Such behavior is surely the epitome of cynicism, and if our students display disquieting evidence of becoming increasingly cynical, we have ourselves and our indefensible practices largely to blame. With grades we *teach* them cynicism, to say nothing of lying, cheating, competitive throat-cutting, and other reprehensible practices.

The Farce Called "Grading"

"But," objects somebody, "after all, a grade is just a sort of *estimate*, and most teachers try to be fair and accurate in their estimates." Yes; most teachers try to be fair and accurate, but all the time they know—at least, those who are honest with themselves know—that they are attempting the impossible. No self-respecting teacher ever rests peacefully the night after turning in a set of grades, for he knows that the "system" has made a charlatan of him and he goes to bed hating himself for it. And as for the estimate, let us not disregard the fact that an *absolute* pass-or-fail system has no place for estimates. Is that 87 on your test paper an estimate? If it is, then mightn't it really be 88, or 86, or something else? Is that B-minus an estimate? No, indeed; when the reports come out, when the averages and grade-points are computed, when the failures are determined, when you are called in and told that you've flunked out of school, there is no room for estimates—this is a very *absolute* decision.

Incidentally, no teacher I know—myself included, God wot—can explain the precise difference between a B-minus and a C-plus, to say nothing of 60 and 59—or, for that matter, 60 and 59.999999999999.

"But," objects somebody else, "if grades are eliminated, what can we substitute for them?" This inevitable question reminds me of the books that have been written on the subject of how to stop smoking. Such a book can be written in one word: Quit!

We have had this asinine practice of grading in

schools for so long that we unconsciously assume it to be necessary to the learning process, but this is a manifestly false assumption. Grades are one aspect of the artificial paraphernalia which we have deliberately superimposed upon education—along with courses, academic credit, "promotion," degrees, diplomas, certificates, commencement exercises, graduation, faculty rank, and so on *ad infinitum, ad nauseam.*

We hold these minatory requirements over the students because we assume that most of them are naturally lazy, stupid dolts who must somehow be coerced, cajoled, persuaded, threatened, strong-armed into learning what we have decided is "good for them." Much of this required material is dull, boring, meaningless, and will be forgotten almost immediately; and the way it is taught is even worse, but students realize that they must perforce jump through the hoops in order to emerge finally with that coveted degree, that beribboned diploma upon which our society places such high value. What we invariably seem to forget is that this superimposed academic apparatus is not at all intrinsic to learning —not at all a *sine qua non* of education, formal or informal. *It is there because we put it there.* Just because we're accustomed to it, let us not delude ourselves into assuming that it is essential, organic or integral; it isn't. But once it becomes an established system, students often shift their motivations and values and begin to "work for grades." And when we talk to them about "earning" and "deserving" marks, we are only compounding this felony.

The Farce Called "Grading"

There have been successful attempts to eliminate marks. The Danish Folk High Schools and other brave experimental schools have gotten along very well without them. In place of report cards or transcripts covered with cabalistic symbols, written reports and parent-teacher (or parent-teacher-student) conferences are sometimes used to facilitate communication and understanding. For example, employers of young people find descriptive comments about such traits as dependability, resourcefulness, intelligence, honesty, ability to get along with others, and so on, much more meaningful than the conventional academic transcripts of prospective employees. If you were such an employer, would you prefer, on the one hand, a thoughtful evaluation from adults who have observed the young people closely over a period of time, or, on the other hand, an official piece of paper informing you about a C-minus in English History and a B-plus in College Algebra?

Students themselves are so conditioned to grading that they soon become willing dupes of the system. They go to their instructors and ask, "How am I doing in this course?" But in most cases they already *know* how they are doing—better than the instructor does—and the fact that they ask the question demonstrates the unreliability of the system.

Some years ago I found a small midwestern town in which the editor of the local weekly newspaper regularly printed on its front pages the complete names and marks of all the children in that town's schools each time report cards were issued. This editor was obviously a sick man who needed immediate confinement in an institution, but his problem is illustrative of the pathology endemic to the practice of grading. Its elimination is more than I dare hope for in my lifetime,* but until the cancer is rooted out and destroyed we can hope for little real improvement in American education.

* As William Clark Trow observes, "Marks . . . deserve to be abolished. Anyone who has not lived his life in the ivory tower, however, knows that trying to abolish them would be like trying to abolish money."

6

The Folly of Faculty Rank

All men are created equal.
THOMAS JEFFERSON: Declaration of Independence

R.H.I.P.—Rank Has Its Privileges.
ANONYMOUS "FULL" PROFESSOR

ONE OF THE MOST HALLOWED of our academic traditions in higher education is the practice of designating faculty members according to a quasi-military rank system. There are regularly four basic grades in the ascending order of this hierarchy: Instructor, Assistant Professor, Associate Professor, and Professor. In addition, variations like Lecturer, Adjunct Professor, and so on have inevitably accrued in the course of time, with the inexorable operation of Parkinson's Law and with the increasing size and complexity of higher institutions.

Having saddled themselves with this gratuitous system, the panjandrums of academe have long since forgotten that it is not integral to their work. On the contrary, questions of academic rank and promotion have become vital to the professional career of the college faculty member. Such crucial matters as salary and tenure are associated with rank, and the fateful words, "Up or out," have often frozen the marrow of many a nonpublishing young faculty member. If he does not get himself promoted within a specified number of years, he'd better look around for another job.

This entire syndrome is a tremendous waste of time and energy which could very well be otherwise utilized to bring about sorely needed improvements in higher education. Department chairmen and deans spend endless hours conferring about these questions and preparing elaborate dossiers for those

The Folly of Faculty Rank

staff members whom they consider "worthy" of being presented for promotion. The amount of politicking, favor-currying, chicanery, back-slapping, back-stabbing, jealousy and general malice associated with faculty rank and promotion presents a sorry spectacle indeed, especially when indulged in by supposedly learned men whose public image is one of wisdom and magnanimity.

A colleague of mine who had somehow achieved the highest rank in spite of extremely limited ability and competence—and this happens much more often than we would be willing to admit—once said to me, with a "Let's see you try to answer this one" air, "I'll be willing to have rank abolished and give up my professorship when you, sir, are willing to give up your deanship." He missed the point, of course, for deanships, like presidencies, vice-presidencies, and the like, are not academic ranks but administrative titles and therefore discrete. Indeed, it is customary for such administrators to hold professorships in their areas of academic specialization in addition to the titles indicating their responsibilities in the administration, and matters like tenure are associated with the academic rather than the administrative designation.

One of the most commonly heard objections to abolition of this rank (sic!) system is that salary ranges are conveniently associated with the various gradations. But in many institutions the ranges are so broad and overlapping that it is not unusual for the highest paid Assistant Professor, for example, to receive more than the lowest "Full" Professor—who is two jumps ahead of him in rank. If the system were abolished, on what basis would faculty salaries be determined? I humbly suggest *merit*.

Some defenders of the status quo might assert that this is already the case, but any honest denizen of the academic jungle knows better. The highest ranks hold many a nincompoop, while on the other hand we all know Assistant Professors who are good teachers and competent scholars but who blush unseen in their lowly station because they don't publish, or because their department chairman doesn't like them—perhaps he perceives them as threats to his suzerainty over his petty empire. Faculty ranks, like school marks, do far more harm than good; if we professors had half as much sense and courage as we like to be credited with, we would abolish the system forthwith.

Let it be noted that a few brave institutions have done just that, and have not only survived—much to the amazement and chagrin of the old-line rank-worshippers—but are prospering and determined not to revert to such deleterious practices.

7

National Assessment
of Education

National assessment of educational progress would involve programs of tests of elementary and high school pupils to see how good education is throughout the country *and how areas and communities compare.*

NEWSPAPER ITEM (*italics added*)

Although labeled "assessment" program, the . . . project is a national testing program and as such it will be coercive, it will inevitably lead to the pressures of regional, state, and local comparisons, and it will have national overtones in the dispensing of federal aid. . . . [It] would yield very little, if any, information on the performance of students in public and private schools which is not already known.

AMERICAN ASSOCIATION OF SCHOOL ADMINISTRATORS

THE IDEA OF A NATIONAL ASSESSMENT of education appeals to many people. It suggests to them that we will thus determine how well our tremendous investment in our schools is "paying off," whether we are getting "value received" for our tax dollar, and this practical kind of evaluation makes sense to the general public and particularly to the influential, quality-control-minded business man.

The project, supported by the United States Office of Education and sponsored by the Carnegie Corporation, involves the application of "measuring instruments" (authorities are careful to avoid using the word "tests") to voluntary samplings of the school-age and adult population in various geographical regions of the country. At first the samplings will include nine areas: reading, writing, literature, vocational education, fine arts, social studies, mathematics, citizenship and science; and at three levels: what 90 per cent of the population should know, what the majority of the population should know, and what a small (10 per cent) percentage should know.

There are great and obvious dangers in this proposal. In the first place, it concentrates on the *cognitive* side of education to the neglect of the affective and conative aspects. This limitation is built in, of course, because it is relatively less difficult to assay what one *knows* than what one *is* and *wants to be*. But even at best, experts realize that the design of

40

National Assessment of Education

valid and reliable instruments purporting to evaluate knowledge is extremely difficult, and experience in this area tends to build up a healthy skepticism among honest practitioners.

In addition to difficulty and complexity, there is the question of the use to which "results" will be put. We Americans are obsessed by "ratings"—in politics, in television and the arts, in athletics, in many aspects of life—and in this preoccupation with comparisons (most of them quite unscientific and merely expressions of personal opinion) we over-generalize on the results. We use them to "prove" whatever appeals to us, and this is a dangerous practice.

Critics of the program assert that inevitably instructors "will teach for the tests" because of the pressures of comparisons and individual ratings.

The fact that the American Association of School Administrators opposes the assessment has been seized upon by their opponents as proof that the members of that group are afraid of being "exposed" by the program's disclosures. It is a favorite parlor sport in the upper reaches of society today to make game of the schoolmen, to deride them as dolts, asses, anti-intellectuals, Philistines, glorified coaches. There is, of course, some justification for this attitude; for that matter, what professional group is free of incompetents and charlatans—the physicians? The lawyers? The architects? The engineers? The clergy? The journalists? But it is the school administrators who usually bear the brunt of our disapproval and obloquy.

The odious comparisons which will certainly follow upon this national "branding" will have overtones of many kinds. All of us know how eagerly we seize upon such "data" to support our pet arguments and establish the superiority of one group or town or theory or school over another. What matter that the basic evaluation is extremely suspect and fails to take into account all the significant factors? We blithely ignore this ineluctable fact and proceed to argue from the decisions in order to denigrate our particular "pet peeves."

There is also the bugaboo of conformity. Many of those who have unthinkingly opposed public education as tending to "level down," to over-standardize, to create inflexible norms, will now support this endeavor which, more than anything else, could do that very thing. Do we want and need a national standard? This question the American people must answer, in its fullest and most significant aspects.

Most people, being extremely naïve about education, will not understand the statement by Ralph W. Tyler, head of the assessment program, that "no individual student or teacher can make a showing. No student will take more than a small fraction of the exercises. No scores will be obtained on his performance. He will not be assessed at any later time and can gain no desired end, like admission to college or a scholarship." All these negatives will only serve to confuse and frustrate unsophisticated supporters of the program.

There is also (and here I speak particularly to the conservatives) the matter of cost. The assessments are to take place every three to five years, and each will require an expenditure of two to three million dollars. Can we afford to provide this sum for what might prove to be a "pig in a poke?"

A
TENURE

8

Higher Education Discovers the "Lower" Schools

The theory and practice of public education, the training of future teachers and administrators, and the development of elementary and secondary curriculums have traditionally existed in singular isolation from other public institutions and even from other bodies of professional knowledge. . . . [But now] physicists, mathematicians, and biologists are engaged in revamping the highschool curriculum.

JESSE BURKHEAD

Around 1960 our enemies arose from the dead and began to chatter and mumble about scholarship, liberal education, high standards, excellence, education for the gifted, and other shibboleths and rebaked ideas of former generations of so-called upholders of standards. Critics, self-appointed, self-anointed, self-trained, poured forth their ideas, their opinions, their laments. Legislatures heard the critics; foundations subsidized the critics, editors became authorities on every aspect of education; reporters became authorities. Everyone agreed that everything in education—present and past—was wrong, erroneous, muddled, stultifying, degrading.

EDGAR B. WESLEY

UNTIL SOME TIME AFTER WORLD WAR II the existence, influence and importance of elementary and secondary schools were largely ignored by the lordly professors in their ivory towers, except for occasional complaints about the "poorly prepared products" who showed up in their classrooms. Many years ago George S. Counts pointed out—with the hearty concurrence of no less an authority than historian Charles A. Beard—that the scholars who had written the histories of our country had paid little, if any, attention to the great institution of common schools and their significance. Indeed, in 1954 a distinguished committee of American historians meeting in conference under the auspices of the Ford Foundation's Fund for the Advancement of Education, unanimously agreed that ". . . relative to its importance in the development of American society, the history of educational forces in this country both in and out of the schoolroom had been shamefully neglected by American historians. It was also the firm belief of the conference that imperfect knowledge of this history had affected adversely the planning of curricula, the formulation of policy, and the administration of educational agencies in the continuing crisis of American education." Thus did such men as Paul H. Buck, Merle Curti, Francis Keppel, and Arthur M. Schlesinger collectively accept the primary responsibility for many of the deficiencies usually blamed upon elementary and secondary schools.

Higher Education Discovers "Lower" Schools

Among those who viewed this conversion with a jaundiced eye was Edgar B. Wesley, himself an eminent historian of education. In 1966 he pointed out: "The historians have dodged, and still do, the consideration of education for fear they will be labelled educators. . . . Dear colleagues, don't be deceived or misled. The scholars did not write a good textbook in physics; they have not written good programs in mathematics; they have degraded the teaching of English; they have some good, but scattered, non-sequential ideas in the social studies; and the historians have so muddled world history that no one knows what it is about. I tell you the scholars are ignorant. They can lead us only in repeating the errors of the past. Denounce them, proclaim our competence, assert the superiority of teachers and educators over scholars. Pray that this dark night of blind leadership will pass and that the sun of light may shine again as it was shining up to the moment when some great scholar shouted 'Excellence.' " *

Over the years the historians have not been alone in adopting an attitude of condescension toward the "lower" schools and the teachers therein. Representatives of other disciplines and fields of learning have been similarly guilty. Even now it is common for professors of music and art, for instance, to disparage their colleagues who are designated as "music educators" or "art educators," the implication being that the latter, in their preoccupation with preparation of teachers for the elementary and

* It was Elbert Hubbard who said, many years ago, "Now owls are not really wise—they only look that way. The owl is a sort of college professor."

secondary schools, are somehow less respectable than their critical brethren who daintily shudder at the thought of sullying their artistic hands with such menial work, preferring instead to concentrate on what they call "creativity" and "performance" —as if these qualities were intrinsically foreign to teaching itself and the tremendously important task of teacher preparation.

Associations of professors of mathematics, foreign languages and other subjects have recently shown great interest in programs of preparation for elementary and secondary school teachers, including the ever-present problem of state certification. This latter process is intended to ensure that teachers at these levels shall have professional preparation in the teaching act in addition to substantive study in teaching fields. But no such legal guarantee exists at the college level—including junior and community colleges in Illinois and many other states. Perceptive observers of the American educational scene have been pointing out over the years that college and university teaching is the only major professional field in which would-be practitioners need demonstrate not the slightest competence in their profession. Such competence is ordinarily assumed from possession of the doctorate. ("Anyone who knows his stuff can teach it.") The utter falsity of this assumption is attested to by generations of students suffering under the mass incompetence perpetrated by such complete disregard of teaching ability.

A classic example of the higher-lower school confrontation occurred in San Francisco in 1959–60. As a result of considerable controversy over the city's public schools ("galloping progressivism" and "anti-intellectualism" were among the charges) the city's Board of Education arranged for a curriculum survey by eight university professors. The four from the University of California came from departments of English, Economics, Mathematics, and Chemistry, and those from Stanford came from English, Mathematics, History, and Biological Sciences. The study fee of $10,000 was divided equally among the eight, and $2,000 more was provided for various expenses. Their report appeared nine months after their service began.

Almost anyone well acquainted with the attitudes and biases of typical "liberal arts" professors could have written the report for them. In effect, in many ways they predictably advocated turning the elementary and secondary schools into lower colleges. Criticizing what they called "indifference to . . . intellect," they recommended the adoption of such practices as complete ability grouping at all levels, separate curricular "tracks" (academic, commercial, industrial arts, general) in the high schools, a longer school day, a "systematically phonetic method" of teaching reading, city-wide competitive examinations, more emphasis on "basic learning" and less on "education for life in democracy," and more recognition for academic achievement through honor rolls, awards, and so on.

Reactions to the report could have been expected. Arthur Foshay, then president of the Association for Supervision and Curriculum Development, wrote, "The report is a mixture of incisiveness and vagueness, insightfulness and grotesque ignorance. What

[it] does is to prescribe a curriculum that might be suitable in part for a small fraction of the children, if it were properly developed."

On the other hand, the *Bulletin* of the reactionary Council for Basic Education hailed the survey with the prediction that it would "have a greater impact on California, and possibly American education, than half a dozen pretentious conferences or committees. . . . This may be the first major step in restoring to scholars a role in determining conduct and content in public education."

The city's superintendent of schools, a knowledgeable, experienced and diplomatic man, expressed appreciation for the report, agreed with its emphasis on high academic standards (!), commented favorably upon many of its proposals for secondary schools (some of which were already under way before the professors moved in), and minimized greatly its importance for elementary education. ("[The surveyors'] lack of training and proficiency in elementary education has prevented them from being of major assistance at this level," he tactfully wrote.)

He also pointed out that no less than twenty of their recommendations dealt with conditions "outside the immediate control of the local Board of Education." Several of them, he patiently explained, were downright illegal, being contrary to state requirements and the legal Code. Others involved major budget appropriations, and these he pointedly referred to the Board of Education.

Several professional commissions and associations prepared a reply to the survey report, claiming that "the philosophy of education advocated in [it] is so contrary to the public education developed in America that it constitutes a reactionary proposal which could endanger hard-won improvements in public school operation. . . . [The professors appear to] take no responsibility for citizenship education or for moral and spiritual values. . . . When a small number of university professors, or any group with limited, special interests, attempts to determine the public school program best fitted to serve all youth, it clearly is outside the field in which it has special competence. Critics of public education, however well-meaning and sincere, if uninformed about the desires of the community for its schools and about the many practical problems of maintaining such schools, can be just as harmful as if they deliberately set out to disrupt and undermine the schools. . . . The Report cannot by any scholarly definition be called a 'study.' There is no evidence of research design, of careful collection of data, of checking to verify conclusions. It is difficult to reconcile the concern the professors express for scholarship and excellence among public school pupils with the careless and even capricious manner in which their assignment from the . . . Board of Education was handled. The report reflects little but the *opinions* of the writers."

QUERY: *Did the Board of Education and the taxpayers of San Francisco get their money's worth?*

Verily, the professorial mountain did labor and bring forth a twelve-thousand-dollar mouse.

UNIVERSITY
ENGLISH
MATH
LANGUAGE
PSYCHOLOGY
EDUCATION
ART
ENGINEERING
THEATRE
MUSIC

9

The Illiberal "Liberal Arts"

*Hence you see why "liberal studies" are so called; it
is because they are studies worthy of a free-born
gentleman. But there is only one really liberal study,
—that which gives a man his liberty.*

SENECA

*There is nothing intrinsically liberal about English,
foreign languages, or the social sciences. The central
question is not what subjects are pursued,* but how
they are taught. *In order to teach subjects liberally,
every professor needs to be something of a generalist.
The college professor who is worth his salt needs to
know a great deal about a great many things.*
COLLEGE AND UNIVERSITY BULLETIN (*italics added*)

TRADITIONALLY, liberal education is that education befitting the free man. It is broad and foundational rather than specialized and technical, and it is achieved, we are told, by the study of what are designated as the liberal arts. This term carries great prestige in higher education; in a university the liberal arts college is generally regarded as the core of the undergraduate program, and the old-line independent liberal arts colleges are commonly reputed to be the finest of our collegiate institutions.

But here again, as in so many other aspects of education, we constantly engage in wishful thinking and self-delusion. For this is the age of specialization, and specialization is antithetical to liberal education's emphasis on breadth and integration.

Our higher institutions are typically organized on a departmental basis, and the departments tend to be identified and congruent with the traditional academic disciplines such as history, mathematics, English language and literature, foreign languages, the sciences, and so on. And this is where specialization rears its ugly head, and breadth and generality recede into virtual invisibility.*

Robert M. Hutchins puts it this way: "The heart of the modern American university is the depart-

* "The structure of a modern university, with its departmental separations, and its total lack of order among specialized disciplines, represents perfectly the disunity and chaos of modern culture." MORTIMER J. ADLER

ment. It is concerned only with its own specialty. Nobody can control it. I am unaware of any instance in history of a department voluntarily sacrificing its special interests for the sake of the university as a whole. A department has, in fact, no knowledge of the university. It sees other departments as rivals in the competition for money, students, and prestige."

The internecine wars resulting from departmental empire-building and self-aggrandizement present an ignoble spectacle indeed. Professors achieve recognition through a highly specialized process beginning with the Ph.D. "union card"; they write their books and articles and present papers at professional meetings on highly specialized topics; they acquire scholarly reputations and achieve academic promotions in a vicious circle swirling them ever onward into increasing preciosity. They are identified by "field" of specialization and are discouraged from forming any opinions or making any judgments outside of their "field." And all this in the name of liberal education! A sorry spectacle, indeed.

In the past few decades some American universities have attempted to serve the purposes of general education by establishing lower undergraduate level programs known variously as "General College," "Basic College," "University College," or "General Studies." The incoming freshman usually enters this unit and remains there for two years or so without "declaring a major" until he is about to move into upper-division work. The attempt to emphasize broad, general education is typically achieved by eschewing the traditional departmental designations and adopting instead such subject-matter categories as "Man's Physical Environment and Biological Inheritance," "Man's Social Inheritance and Social Responsibilities," "Man's Insights and Appreciations," "Organization and Communication of Ideas," and "Health and Physical Development." These rubrics obviously comprehend broadly what is commonly subsumed under liberal arts and sciences, plus the fine arts, physical education and other nonprofessional subjects.

Now these nontraditional terms are admirable euphemisms, commendably comprehensive, and they look fine in catalogues and bulletins. We spend hours in faculty meetings arguing about requirements in each category, or whether one of them (the last of those listed above, naturally!) should be eliminated entirely. But *what happens in the classrooms?* Do our highly specialized faculty instructors in these programs completely reorient their approaches, techniques, course outlines, tests and examinations, and so on, so as to achieve the breadth and integration for which the entire program exists? *C'est à rire.*

In the first place, most professors resist such programs and submit to their imposition only unwillingly and rebelliously, while in actuality they simply rename the same old courses, tinker with the organization a bit, reduce the credit hours and perhaps drop some feature like laboratory work, and blithely go on still doing business at the same old stand but under another name. They are understandably pleased when the top administration assures them

The Illiberal "Liberal Arts"

that no separate faculty will be established to teach these "general" courses (and that, indeed, in institutions where this was done the program invariably failed and was dropped). Professors are notoriously possessive and jealous of their ownership rights, and such assurances feed their vanity and self-image. And so, with a few minor adjustments, they go on doing what they've always been doing. If it's under an assumed name, what matter? After some grumbling, peace returns to the campus.

But let's not deceive ourselves. The fact remains that the highly specialized and rigidly habituated approach of the typical professor means that virtually the entire concept of generality will be subverted anyway; the fancy program will exist only on paper, while pretty much the same old tired thing goes on in the classrooms. In other words, if such programs are to achieve their laudable objectives, the instructors must indeed be *different* in that they must themselves be broadly educated, dedicated to the integrative principles underlying the program, and (dare I say it?) *effective teachers*. Somewhere such a rare bird can be found, perhaps. I'd like to run across one some day.

Realistically, of course, we must recognize that such general programs can provide a convenient *Gestalt* for rationalizing the practice of herding groups of hundreds of undergraduates into vast lecture halls where they slump somnolescently while the lecturer's voice drones on from the podium. Too often we forget that what transpires in classrooms may be a far cry from what is suggested and implied in the glittering rhetoric of a school's catalogues and publicity materials.

Every educational institution would do well to heed Harold Taylor's warning: "The first task of education is not, as is generally assumed, to teach the subject-matter of the arts and sciences. It is to raise the level of awareness and response to *all* ideas, events, people and objects. If there is a narrow range of possibility in the area of response—a uniformity of ideas, people, objects, events—then the level of awareness remains comparably low, the education itself becomes narrowing in its effects."

10

The "Academicians"
and the "Educationists"

I assume that . . . professors [of philosophy, political science, history] are both reasonably informed about the schools and concerned with the bearing of their discipline on educational problems. I must say, however, that this assumption is not yet met by many of these professors.

JAMES BRYANT CONANT

The professional educator has been the sacrificial object of crusading zealots for the one right educational approach. In order to differentiate him from other teachers in institutions of higher learning, who have happily awakened to the realization that they, too, are educators, despite the fact that precious few of them have even thought hard or consistently about education, the professional educator has been dubbed an "educationist." This ugly word has acquired a certain disparaging connotation. An "educationist" is one who without knowing very much about any particular subject matter teaches the teachers of our children how to teach without overmuch concern whether our children really learn anything of consequence.

SIDNEY HOOK

UNDERGRADUATE STUDENTS entering my classroom are sometimes greeted by the following list already written on the blackboard:

> Mickey Mouse
> Rinky-dink
> Trivial
> Inflated
> Overlapping
> Repetitious
> Anti-intellectual
> Dull and boring
> Lacking "challenge"
> Busy-work

When I ask the students what these terms describe, the answer is immediately forthcoming: "Education courses!" In making this identification they are reflecting the stereotype which is common on our campuses—that courses in professional Education are all this and more, a waste of time, an insult to the intelligence. (David Boroff says, "It is, of course, fashionable for students everywhere to heap contumely on Education courses.")

But my classroom exercise does not stop there. After a short analysis of the implications, I proceed to assert, "Now, of course these terms on the blackboard apply *only* to Education courses, for all of your other courses are just the opposite."

At this point the change of expression on the

"Academicians" and "Educationists"

faces of many of the students is often striking; they are obviously going through a new experience, a new internalization. Slowly, reluctantly, they begin to admit that Education courses certainly have no monopoly upon these critical descriptions; they agree with Paul Woodring who said, "There is a certain amount of humbug, propaganda, and bad guesswork in some courses in sociology, economics, literary criticism, anthropology, physics, and almost everything else listed in the college catalogue." Confronted by their hypocrisy, the students usually excuse themselves by saying, "Everybody else talks like this about Education courses—especially the non-Education professors. To some extent we pick it up from them." Then I ask them whether they believe that "the best defense is a good offense"—that you can more easily disguise your own defects and inadequacies if you concentrate on pointing out the other fellow's, whether real or imaginary.

This exercise in truth-confrontation serves to point up an unfortunate and uncritical assumption which is widely held on our campuses, to the effect that Education in the professional sense is somehow quite separate and distinct from the traditional fields of learning comprehended in the conventional arts-and-sciences curricula. Thus we hear the "scholars," on the one hand, contrasted with the "educationists," on the other.

It is true, of course, that Schools / Colleges of Education are professional units, charged with a special function and not to be thought of, or treated, as some kind of pale, not-quite-respectable imitations or parallels of the hoary arts-and-sciences units. Their purposes are quite different; the latter's is broad and general, while the former's is more specific and task-oriented. The Education unit should provide the best possible *professional* program of teacher preparation; it should also carry on continuing study and research in all aspects of the professional field and should strive to relate formal education to its cultural milieu.

But let us not forget that the professional school builds upon the base provided by the preprofessional unit. Students preparing to teach ordinarily take a small fraction of their total program in professional Education. It is customary to refer to the "academic disciplines" on the one hand, and to "Education courses," on the other; but this is an inexact and invidious distinction, for if the "disciplines" are "academic," then by inference Education is nonacademic—not to say a nondiscipline. By conforming in this practice, we help to perpetuate the fiction that the academicians sit among the blessed, and the educationists among the damned. The entire syndrome is unrealistic and deleterious; it does incalculable harm to our total educational enterprise.

Among the academicians who in recent years have turned their attention to professional Education are James Bryant Conant and James D. Koerner. Conant's book entitled *The Education of American Teachers* is an earnest, conscientious work, but as George S. Counts points out, it might better have been called *The Certification of American Teachers*. Koerner's book, *The Miseducation of*

American Teachers, is more outspoken than Conant's; he includes a scathing denunciation of the Education classes which he visited and textbooks which he reviewed in preparing his diatribe. In reviewing it, Paul Woodring astutely pointed out: "Not many professors of *any* subject would care to have their work evaluated on the basis of a fifty-minute visit by a hostile critic whose low opinion of the subject being taught was on record long before the visit."

Both Conant and Koerner are critical of courses in philosophy of education, history of education, educational psychology, and so on, on the basis that these courses too often are taught, and the textbooks written, by people not well enough trained in philosophy, history, psychology, or whatever. Speaking of the textbooks, Koerner claims (without foundation, in most cases), "One [notices] the scarcity of recognized authors. Like the textbooks used in public schools, the authors are generally educationists of no particular reputation, and of no scholarly standing whatever."

This incessant dichotomization is pointless and harmful to our educational purposes. Obviously, no group is free from charlatans and incompetents. Obviously, teachers at all levels should be scholars, well versed in their teaching fields. And just as obviously, scholars in the classroom need to be competent teachers—but this latter point is almost completely ignored by the academician-critics.

Sidney Hook, an eminent philosopher and certainly no "educationist," says, "The professional educators have been denounced as 'self-serving par-agons of mediocrity,' who have imposed patterns of accreditation on the various local educational sys-tems, making it impossible for teachers of the young to exercise their craft unless they enroll in certain prescribed courses in pedagogy. These courses are often characterized as irrelevant if not detrimental to a genuine teaching process whose fruits should be the acquisition of the skills of communication, famil-iarity with the cultural heritage of our civilization, and basic knowledge of the major intellectual disci-plines. . . . However, it makes much less sense to criticize Schools or Departments of Education for failing to teach the subject matter of the conven-tional disciplines, which is not their primary prov-ince, than to criticize liberal arts colleges or depart-ments, which should have the chief responsibility for instruction in such courses, for failing to teach subject-matter courses properly. It is notorious that ability to teach, or even knowledge of the barest rudiments of good teaching, is not regarded as a prerequisite for teaching in the overwhelming ma-jority of liberal arts institutions of the country."

Unless and until we develop many more genuine scholar-teachers for our classrooms at *all* levels, American education will not be as good as it should be and must be.

11

The Vanishing "Teachers College"

*Teachers colleges found it difficult to gain accep-
tance in the academic world because both university professors and the public at large identified
them with the normal schools out of which they had
grown, and normal schools were not a part of
higher education.*

PAUL WOODRING

*Teachers of the future will not be admitted to pro-
fessional training until they have completed a
considerable amount of liberal education at the
college level, and for many this will mean a liberal
arts degree before the first professional degree.
Teacher education will no longer be a thing apart
but will be an integral part of higher education.*

PAUL WOODRING

HISTORICALLY, "teachers colleges" have been a highly visible and much maligned member of the confraternity of American education. One of my colleagues, an internationally known scientist, once said to me, with considerable feeling, "Teachers colleges stink!" *Sic transit* scientific objectivity.

Teachers colleges arose primarily because of the tremendous need for large numbers of professionally prepared teachers to staff the rapidly increasing schoolrooms of this burgeoning country. Most of these institutions were separate and state-supported; a few were components of major universities; there were other variations such as the now obsolete (or at least obsolescent) "county normals" and still other special types. At the same time, of course, large numbers of teachers—especially for high schools—came (and still come) out of the traditional liberal arts colleges; and most universities, both public and private, established units known as Schools (or Colleges) of Education to assume responsibility for the professional aspects of preparing teachers for elementary and secondary schools and to carry on the study of education as social process.

Today we see a shift in the predominant nomenclature. Most of the erstwhile "teachers colleges" and "normal schools" are changing their names to State Colleges or State Universities and deliberately cultivating a multi-purpose image.

And—let's face it—much of this drive for pres-

The Vanishing "Teachers College"

tige stems from the impression implicit in my scientist colleague's contemptuous opinion quoted above: Teachers colleges have for years been regarded in most academic circles as innately inferior to liberal arts colleges and have been "low men on the academic totem pole."

Now, all this name-changing is quite understandable and certainly important, in view of our previously mentioned tendency to operate in terms of catchwords and clichés. However, most people fail to realize—and I have never seen it recognized clearly in the voluminous literature now extant—that, to a certain extent, teachers colleges *are* liberal arts colleges, and liberal arts colleges *are* teachers colleges.

Let my shocked and indignant audience read on. After all, the programs of preparation for teaching in our American elementary and secondary schools consist of two main parts. The first (theoretically, at least) is a broad foundation in general education, which is primarily "liberal arts and sciences," plus some specialization in depth in one or two teaching fields. (Incidentally, the term "teaching field" is far more significant and useful for professional purposes than are the traditional terms "major" and "minor.")

Since elementary school teachers typically work with their pupils over large blocks of time and in various areas of basic skills, the preparation of such teachers tends to emphasize breadth, with much attention to the dynamic, affective, noncognitive aspects of dealing with the very young, especially in the socialized classroom setting. Even here, to be sure, many of the more conservative critics of teacher education (few of whom, to my knowledge, have ever successfully tried teaching a class of children) insist that the traditional major-minor pattern of preparation is proper for such teachers, too.

Secondary schools are usually departmentalized and the teachers identified by their curricular teaching fields (or "subjects") most of which are generally congruent with the traditional liberal arts disciplines: English, mathematics, science, foreign language, the social sciences—plus others in business and commercial subjects, vocational-technical work, physical education and "special" areas such as art, music, and dramatics.

The second component in teacher preparation—and this is where lips begin to curl and noses to wrinkle—is a required program in the *professional* aspects of teaching, a program which actually takes up a relatively minor part of the student's total undergraduate work but is required for legal certification to teach. This professional program for teacher preparation usually includes study of such topics as: the school as a social institution, the teaching-learning process, growth and development of children and youth, measurement and evaluation of academic achievement, general and special teaching methods and procedures, and curricular content and patterns. There is often some examination of the historical-philosophical foundations of education, with a new emphasis upon comparative and international education now emerging. This professional

The Vanishing "Teachers College"

program often makes provision for some observation in classrooms, and regularly culminates in a period of actual student-teaching—a kind of practical, on-the-job experience under the supervision of an experienced teacher.

The entire program briefly sketched above makes good sense—at least in theory—to many people and tends to parallel preparatory programs in other professions, but it has long been the object of much criticism—especially, though not entirely, from those who have not themselves been elementary or secondary teachers (college professors, journalists, the military, and business men particularly).

Apart from this criticism, however, it is important to note that many of our teachers have for years come out of the so-called "liberal arts colleges," and obviously any such college admitting students to teacher preparation programs must provide both of the components described above. That is, in addition to its departments based on the time-honored disciplines, it must provide in its curriculum the necessary professional preparation required by state teacher-certification laws. To this extent, then, such liberal arts colleges *are* teachers colleges—not in name, to be sure, but in actual function. Likewise, the so-called teachers colleges must and do provide, in addition to Education courses, the "general education" base plus opportunities for some specialization in depth in the various teaching fields encompassed in our typical "comprehensive" secondary schools. To this extent, then, such teachers colleges *are* liberal arts colleges.

Having said all this, I must hasten to add that the subject has by no means been exhausted. There is much to be said for the effect and influence of an institution's self-image, its basic orientation, the value judgments which it inevitably reflects. Many institutions, acutely aware of the pejorative connotations of the term "teachers college," have tried valiantly to sweep under the rug the fact that large numbers—perhaps even a majority—of their students are preparing to be teachers. Surprisingly often, indeed, this function is the "backbone" of the institution, without which it could not well exist. Among the more recently established universities are a good many formerly named "teachers college" or "normal school." To say that such an institution "used to be a puny teachers college but is now a full-fledged university" (and these are phrases often heard) is but to play down the obvious fact that, although its name has changed and it has acquired the diversity and the many embellishments and trappings commonly associated in people's minds with universities, it continues to perform a major service to the state and nation through the annual preparation of hundreds, or even thousands, of teachers for the elementary and secondary schools, as well as for junior and community colleges; and, furthermore, that were it not for this basic function, the accretive programs—many of them far more glamorous, novel, and headline-worthy—could not have been added or justified.

Likewise, far too often the liberal arts college, uncomfortably aware that many of its students are preparing to go into teaching, and chafing under the legal necessity of recognizing certification requirements, has downgraded the teacher-preparation function to the extent of regarding the faculty members engaged in professional preparation of teachers as second-class citizens, relegating them to the worst buildings, offices, and classrooms (and some of them are pretty bad) and treating them as a necessary evil. It is not unusual for such an institution to hire a nearby available school administrator —perhaps a retired gentleman—to handle all of the professional preparation (teach all of the Education courses, "supervise" the student teaching, and so on)—the college's attitude being that, "as everybody knows, these experiences are trivial, busywork, a waste of time, but we have to provide them because of those thrice-damned certification requirements bootlegged into the legal code by the Educationist Establishment." Under such auspices it is somewhat less than astonishing that the programs are often of poor quality.

Actually, there is much loose talk about "good" and "bad" schools, not only by people in general but also by a surprisingly large number of professionals who should know better. These evaluative comments, often tossed off in cavalier fashion, tend to be highly subjective and over-generalized. We need to rid ourselves of such unscientific rating habits. There are so many different institutions, of so many diverse types and with so much overlapping and specialization, that sharp distinctions and precise evaluations are impossible. There are many spectrums involved; in all probability, many liberal arts colleges are "better" than many others in various ways, just as many teachers colleges, other professional schools, and technical schools are "better" than others, but overall quality ratings are dangerous and misleading.

However, other things being equal, it seems logical that the institution which recognizes (dare we say "welcomes"?) teacher preparation as one of its main functions (and it often is *the* main function) and organizes all its resources to do the best job it possibly can in this area will probably do that job better than one which tries to ignore the function and proceeds to meet minimum requirements unwillingly and reluctantly, dragging its academic feet and cutting corners wherever possible, and pretending that the teacher preparation function doesn't really exist. (Incidentally, this is why some few brave teachers colleges still retain their original name and designation in order to recognize that basic purpose and keep it clear and prominent.) We need far more honesty, rather than hypocrisy, in this as in other areas.

12

The Eradication
of Misinformation

It ain't ignorance that causes all the trouble in this world; it's the things that folks know that ain't so.

JOSH BILLINGS

Misinformation is one of the greatest dangers of modern education.

CHARLES F. KETTERING

IF THESE ESTIMABLE GENTLEMEN ARE RIGHT—
and I suspect that there is more than a modicum of
truth in their statements—they have pointed up a
lamentable state of affairs, and it behooves us as
educators to explore the causes and the remedies
therefor.

How soon in life do people begin to accumulate
their stores of misinformation? At a very early age,
as any observant parent can testify. One need not
listen long to the conversation of children before
detecting evidence of misstatement of fact, incorrect
quotation, generalizing from insufficient data, falla-
cious reasoning, and so on. (For that matter, of
course, the identical foibles are equally discernible
in a good many adults.)

What are the sources of this misinformation?
Needless to say, they are legion. Children sometimes
draw erroneous conclusions from personal observation; they are easily influenced by the statements of
their parents and other well-meaning but often ignorant elders, by the gratuitous assertions of their
playmates, and before long by the authoritarian
character of the instruction they receive in most
educational institutions.

Adults, too, are beset on all sides by superstition
and error. Popular misconceptions are common
(such as, "Lightning never strikes twice in the
same place") and are implicitly believed by the uncritical. Through media of mass communication like

The Eradication of Misinformation

newspapers, movies, radio and television, we are bombarded with exaggeration and distortion, with "slanted" information in the news, with oversimplification of issues in the editorials, with plausible, pseudoscientific claptrap in advertising.

Most adults regard the school as an agency established by society for the primary purpose of imparting information to the young. This frame of reference results in popular emphasis upon the acquisition of subject-matter: Miss Smith is lauded as a good teacher "because she makes you learn" and Jones School is condemned "because you don't learn anything there." Specious judgments like these disregard the true nature of the learning process, for learning of one sort or another goes on willy-nilly, regardless of the efforts of teachers, textbooks and schools to promote or retard it.

How is it possible for schools with their teachers and textbooks to contribute to the average human being's store of misinformation? Think back over your own school days; remember some of those neurotic, prejudiced "characters" to whom your formal education was entrusted and some of the textbooks to which you were subjected. Did your science teacher tell you (as mine did) that water always freezes at 32 degrees Fahrenheit? Did your American history textbooks present an objective, unbiased picture of such topics as the Civil War, our barbarous treatment of the Indians, our relations with the neighboring countries of Canada and Mexico, and our international policies?

How, then, can the school aid in the eradication

of misinformation? To begin with, it must needs take the child as he comes to it, already burdened, even at the tender age of five or six, with a complex of accumulated misconceptions and prejudices. What it does with him—the kind of educational experience it provides for him—will to a great extent determine whether his store of misinformation will continue to increase daily or whether he will develop into a well-informed, enlightened adult.

The kind of educational experience provided for the child must inevitably reflect the school's educational philosophy. Is it completely authoritarian, dispensing ready-made, predigested "truth" for rote memorization and mechanical parroting-back (the process has also been called "regurgitation")? Are unquestioning acceptance and obedience demanded of the child? Such *ipse dixit* methods are reminiscent of what many of us found most reprehensible during military service, where we encountered an obscurantist system which too often ignored the question of intrinsic validity and importance of actions, information and decisions, placing its sole emphasis on the superficial aspects of rank and protocol. (A wartime case is known in which two lieutenant-colonels delayed the transmission of important information over the telephone until they compared "dates of rank" and thus determined which of them would have to address the other as "Sir"!)

It is characteristic of human nature to yearn for fixed truth, for finality. We like to feel that things are settled, that we can depend upon indefinite continuance of the status quo. We associate mutation with depreciation, as in the words of the well-known hymn, "Change and decay in all around I see." And yet we know that change is inevitable and that its effects are not necessarily pejorative per se.

This enduring mutability of all things is particularly reflected in the rapidity of modern technological development. New processes, new syntheses, new interpretations are constantly evolving. The fantastic science fiction of yesterday is today's commonplace actuality. Some books are out of date even before they can be published.

It is only the part of wisdom, then, for us to be wary of dogmatism at any time, from any source. In all fairness to ourselves and our students, let us think critically as individuals and as teachers. Let us apply the scientific method more realistically; let us utilize the tentative hypothesis and be ready to revise and reconstruct when such a procedure is indicated. Let us be properly skeptical of self-constituted authority with its claims to omniscience and infallibility. In confronting error and superstition wherever we find them, let us realize that they are fostered by ignorance and fear, and let us challenge them as they are challenged in the words of the once popular song, "It ain't necessarily so!"

Must such a course of action involve an abnegation of faith? Certainly not; it simply advocates a realistic approach to life and its problems, including the educative process. Through its application both children and adults may succeed in materially reducing their accumulated stores of misinformation,

and that is a consummation devoutly to be wished.*
We see through a glass, darkly. Too many of us
know too many things that aren't so.

* As Benjamin Franklin observed in 1734, "A learned
blockhead is a greater blockhead than an ignorant one,"

13

The Increasing Shortage
of Teachers

*The teacher is the most important factor in good
education [but] in the educational hierarchy he
is low man on the totem pole. In the power structure, he is the one without power. In the line of
order, he is the one who takes orders from everyone
else. He has little chance to exercise creativity, to
show intelligence, or to use democratic procedures.
He has no say in the important decisions affecting
the schools. The educational system in America
today is a vertical hierarchy and the teacher is at
the bottom. There is something terribly wrong
here. . . .*

ANNE MITCHELL

*. . . The teachers in the elementary and secondary
schools [are] still baby sitters.*

ROBERT M. HUTCHINS

WE ARE NOW IN THE THROES of a massive shortage of teachers—the most serious since the days of World War II—and prospects of any significant alleviation are dim indeed. In reality, the scarcity will probably increase in the immediate future, and it is quite possible that our country will ere long face its greatest educational crisis on this very point.

We have lived with this problem, but on a smaller scale, for many years, to be sure. We have attempted to relieve the situation by adopting such emergency measures as temporary certification of college-graduate housewives, retired persons, junior college graduates, and so on. But these undesirable stopgaps have not solved the basic shortage, which has continued to grow year by year.

Preoccupied as we are with wars and rumors of wars, with space travel, with manifold problems at home and abroad, we have not yet faced up to the grave implications of the lack of qualified teaching personnel for our classrooms. But before long the confrontation will be inevitable, and our society will no longer be able to turn away and pretend that the problem isn't there.

The etiology of this crisis is not difficult to trace. Increasing militancy of teachers, with strikes and boycotts such as those recently in Kentucky, Michigan, and New York, has developed primarily because of low salaries and poor working conditions. For many years we have joked about teachers'

The Increasing Shortage of Teachers

"moonlighting" (earning extra money by working at other jobs during evenings, weekends, and so on). In most cases, however, this is an expedient required by a desperate inadequacy in the salary schedule.

But teachers, especially in the elementary and secondary schools, are not only generally underpaid; they are often overworked and saddled with chores inappropriate to their role. Teachers should be *directors of instruction*, not baby-sitters, ticket-sellers, clerks, money-collectors, policemen. They need time and energy for planning, reading, conferring with each other and with students, and many other activities essential to their efficient functioning.

Teaching children is a strenuous undertaking, requiring good health—both physical and mental. Good teachers are usually exhausted at the end of a school day. Fortunately, the profession has many dedicated practitioners who are the backbone of American education, but we need many, many more —and we are not getting them.

Acts of violence by students against teachers are exacerbating an already acute problem. Discourtesy and rowdiness on the part of pupils, switchblade knives and tire chains in the classroom, uniformed police patrolling corridors and lunchrooms in urban schools—conditions such as these are more and more discouraging young people from going into teaching. No self-respecting person will submit to such indignities indefinitely. And let us not delude ourselves into thinking that these are school problems solely: they are problems of our society, just as the schools are a creation and expression of that society.

Teachers need professional status and dignity, good salaries and working conditions, and the respect of both children and adults. With these advantages, our country can have the kind of educational system it so desperately needs. Without them, we face a future fraught with peril. The American people must meet the challenge of providing excellence in all phases of education, or be prepared for the inevitable consequences.

14

Lean's Law of Pedagogy:
Bad Teaching Drives Out Good

What the teacher is, is more important than what he teaches.

KARL MENNINGER

The good teacher is an interesting man or woman. As such, he or she will make the work interesting for the students, in just the same way as he or she talks interestingly and writes an interesting letter.

GILBERT HIGHET

YOUNG MR. BLANK was a successful history teacher, and he loved his work. He had always liked school and enjoyed learning, and after some years of public school teaching, during which time he completed his Master's degree in history at a nearby university, he decided to follow his professors' advice and begin working toward a doctorate.

He was granted a graduate assistantship which called for some undergraduate-level teaching, and this he anticipated eagerly. He "knew his history" and, having had the tremendous advantage (which, unfortunately, very few college professors have) of successful high school teaching experience, he also knew how to create a good classroom atmosphere, how to stimulate discussion, how to motivate his students, how to illustrate difficult points in different ways, how to make judicious use of humor, how to relate the subject to cognate disciplines and to world problems, how to point out practical applications, how to avoid the droning monotony of constant lecturing. The first commandment in his pedagogical Decalogue was: Thou shalt not be DULL. Moreover, he was interested in his students and always more than willing to help them and discuss their problems, of whatever nature.

As a result his students generally liked him and looked forward to his classes; they prepared their work well and learned much. They felt that they were not only learning history and enjoying it, but that their association with Mr. Blank was a worthwhile personal experience—that he taught them more than just history.

They agreed among themselves that his tests were usually rather difficult but that their classwork and study had prepared them adequately, and so most of them achieved quite well. In the list of final grades there were several A's, and about half of the class came out with B's. Mr. Blank felt his usual mild euphoria about it all at term's end, and after the grades were turned in at the departmental office a good many of the students sought him out to express their sincere appreciation to him for helping them to have a pleasant and worthwhile educative experience.

A few weeks later the history department chairman, a rather pompous graybeard who insisted on constantly lecturing to his own students and invariably put most of them to sleep, summoned Mr. Blank into his office. Closing the door and clearing his throat in obvious embarrassment, the professor held up a paper and said, "Uh, Mr. Blank, I feel it my duty to call this matter to your attention. I have here last term's grade distribution list from the registrar's office, and it shows that your classes received somewhat higher grades than the others in the department—and in other departments, too. Now, I do not, of course, wish to dictate to you how to grade your students, but after all, Mr. Blank, we pride ourselves on maintaining high standards in this department and must be careful not to let our courses become known as 'pipes,' or whatever the equivalent word is these days. That would damage the academic respect in which we are held by our colleagues and give us a bad name for 'diluting' our courses and lowering our standards. I'm sure you understand why such a thing must not be allowed to happen."

Mr. Blank had half expected this speech, and he knew better than to attempt any explanation or to defend his practices. An intelligent young man, he realized only too well that he was distinctly in the minority, that the "System" was rigged against good teaching, that the many incompetents all around him prided themselves on their "high standards" when in reality they were using the shibboleth to disguise their own miserably poor teaching.

Still, he was indignant and frustrated, for he saw clearly that much of what passes for "education" in our schools—and especially in colleges and universities—is actually, for the most part, MISeducation perpetrated by ANTIteachers.

But what could he say? Leaving the office in silence, he walked slowly down the corridor, musing over the seeming paradox that the better you teach, the more you are punished by the Establishment which controls your advancement in the profession. He recalled that, on the first day of the term, he had passed the open door of one of the lecture halls and heard the professor say to the class, "I want each of you to take a good look at the student next to you, for by the end of the term one of you will be gone. In this department we are proud that our standards are so high that we flunk fifty per cent of our students."

Lean's Law of Pedagogy

Such a pseudo-teacher, in Mr. Blank's opinion, should be disbarred from the profession, but on the contrary he was considered as a distinguished scholar—hadn't he written several books? Who cared what crimes he perpetrated on the defenseless students in his classes?

Mr. Blank sadly shook his head as he remembered the words of one who was himself a great teacher: "Father, forgive them, for they know not what they do."

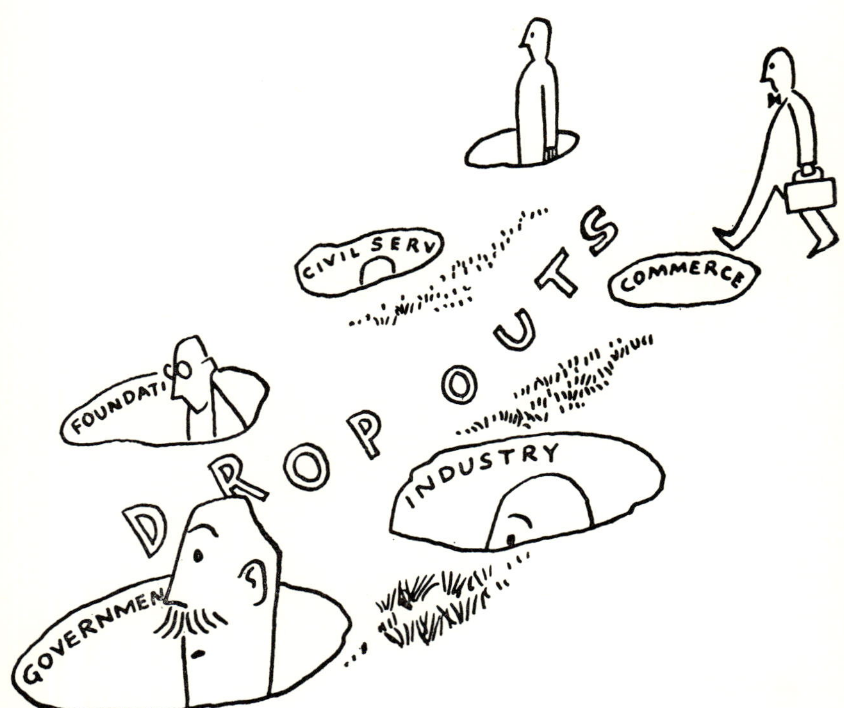

DROPOUTS
CIVIL SERV
COMMERCE
FOUNDATI
INDUSTRY
GOVERNMEN

15

Prescription for American Education

*Human history becomes more and more a race
between education and catastrophe.*

H. G. WELLS

*. . . the present age calls for a great education, for
an education liberally and nobly conceived, for
an education directed toward the accomplishment
of the heavy tasks before us, for an education that
expresses boldly and imaginatively the full promise
and the full strength of America in her historical
and world setting.*

GEORGE S. COUNTS

I DO NOT PROFESS—though I am indeed a professor —to know the remedies for all the manifold ills besetting American education. I am sure, however, that the following steps are necessary if we wish to make any significant improvement in our educational enterprise.

1 Develop a truly professional concept of teaching *at all levels*. Require evidence of competence in teaching for acceptance into the profession. Improve salaries and working conditions for all teachers. Recognize that good teaching is difficult, demanding, and supremely important.

2 Work toward the eventual abolition of marks, faculty ranks, and all other extraneous paraphernalia which currently superimpose gratuitous and crushing burdens upon the schools.

3 Recognize and emphasize the fact that education is more than mechanical memorization and regurgitation of factual information. Strive to eliminate the commodity concept of education.

4 Reverse the currently popular pyramidal concept of "higher" education and the "lower" schools. It is the early years which are by far the most important in the individual's life, so that the education of the "highest" value is that which takes place in the elementary schools.

5 Revise the "liberal arts" programs so as to rid them of their present academic arteriosclerosis and make them truly liberal. This process will require a complete and drastic overhauling of departmental organization, curricular design, preparation of professors, and almost all the trappings now found in most of our colleges and universities.

6 Recognize that teacher preparation is the primary responsibility of the Schools and Colleges of Education, which must be equal partners in the community of scholars. Education in this sense is both a professional program and an academic discipline, not a backdoor interloper.

7 Recognize that *all* institutions preparing teachers are, in effect, "teachers colleges." With that understanding, we can rid ourselves of the puerile and snobbish downgrading which is one of the currently popular academic parlor games.

8 Take a long look at national assessment of education. This program has built-in guarantees of general and widespread misunderstanding and confusion, of which there is far too much already.

9 Do not depend upon the ivory-tower academicians to come up with practical suggestions for the improvement of education at any level. Call upon the

wisest of the professional educators, who have spent the greater part of their lives studying and working in the schools and have thought deeply and broadly about education as social institution and process.

These basic changes, plus others already recommended by astute professionals in the field, must be resolutely made if we are determined not to continue stumbling along under the same handicaps and self-imposed burdens which now impede our progress. Without these changes, it is very difficult to see how we can move forward boldly to achieve the kind of quality education which is worthy of the most powerful nation in the world community.

Index